KINGDOM
LIVING

To my dear friend Min. Vanessa,
May the power of God take
you places you've never
been. May the spirit of God
elevate you to higher
heights in Him.
perpetual blessings,

Patricia DeLoatch

KINGDOM

LIVING | Walking in the Power of God's Word

TATE PUBLISHING *& Enterprises*

Published by Tate Publishing & Enterprises, LLC
127 E. Trade Center Terrace | Mustang, Oklahoma 73064 USA
1.888.361.9473 | www.tatepublishing.com

Tate Publishing is committed to excellence in the publishing industry. The company reflects the philosophy established by the founders, based on Psalm 68:11,
"The Lord gave the word and great was the company of those who published it."

Book design copyright © 2010 by Tate Publishing, LLC. All rights reserved.
Cover design by Kandi Evans
Interior design by Nathan Harmony

Published in the United States of America

ISBN: 978-1-61663-146-8
1. Religion: Christian Life: Spiritual Growth
2. Religion: Chrisitan Life: General
10.04.08

Dedication

I dedicate this book to my heavenly Father. I owe you everything and I want to live my life exercising the gift you placed within me: the gift of teaching your Word of Truth in power and boldness to all that will listen. Father, I owe you me! Thank you for the opportunity to share You in me.

To my earthly father, Raymond Brown. I love you with all my heart, and just in case you didn't know, you are the best father any child could ever have. To my brothers, Steven and Cedric, we are indeed an extension of our wonderful and giving mother, Agnes. I love you both.

To my gifted and loving children, Brittny (and my grandchildren, Morgan and Christian), India, Jason, and Joshua. Thank you for allowing me to do God's work and for reminding me when it's time for just us (yeah, family night)! Mommy loves you all very much.

And last but never least, to the man who knows me and gets me and treats me like a queen—the love of my life, Bill. Thank you for falling in love with me all over again and showing me that there is no failure in nor nothing wasted in God. I love you!

Acknowledgments

A special thanks to Cecelia L. Harris for the foreword and especially for over twenty years of friendship, mentoring, and for genuine agape love. Words cannot express the gratitude I have for you. Although our friendship is numbered by twenty-two, it's as if we have known one another an entire lifetime. You have always known the real me and pushed and coached for the real me to manifest, and for that, I am eternally grateful. My prayer is that I would be half the friend/sister to you that you are to me. We are indeed one in the spirit, just as what was prophesied to us many years ago, and nothing will ever change that.

You are destined by God to fulfill His purpose and plan for your life and to do a great work for Him in His kingdom. I look for great exploits to be done by you and your family in days, weeks, months, and years to come. I love you with the love of Christ.

To the pastors, especially Pastor Mattie H. Johnson, that mentored me and who were responsible for helping shape and mold me into the person I am today—Pastor Calvin Johnson, Bishop Donald and Pastor Vanessa Black, Bishop Emma Dickens, Minister Monica Gattison, and Pastor Eunice Meade.

I would be remised to neglect the Sisterhood and Fresh Anointing Ministries, my prayer groups. Ladies, you have all been an inspiration to me in more ways than you can imagine. I love you all.

A heartfelt thank you goes out to all my family (my aunts, uncle, mother-in-law, sister-in-laws, nephews, nieces, godchildren, and my adopted spiritual children), extended family (Ms. Hastie), and friends. You all have touched me in a very special way, and that is why we are connected.

Also, a special thank you to the entire Tate Publishing family for your prayers and diligent work on this project.

Table of Contents

Foreword	11
Point One: What Love Is	15
Point Two: What Love Made You	29
Point Three: The Kingdom of God	45
Point Four: Thy Kingdom Come	55
Point Five: A Life of Compassion	65
Point Six: A Life of Holiness	75
Point Seven: Thy Will Be Done	87

Foreword

By Cecelia L. Harris

We started as partners in crime. Well, when we first met, we both had not yet experienced the transformation of life that takes place when one receives the gift of salvation. It was the summer of 1987, and we were living our lives by the world's standards. We were participating in the pleasures of this world without regard for standards of holiness. Partners in crime, we were—sinners. Over the next several years, we both would experience the soulful hurts and pains associated with death, divorce, and other major life disappointments. Together, we would also celebrate the birth of Patricia's daughter and my goddaughter, India. We would eventually be baptized at the same time as well. Now, partners in Christ—redeemed, saved.

Our trials did not end because we accepted Jesus as Lord and Savior. We continued to experience the peaks and valleys of life as we learned how to grow spiritually through study and application of God's word. What we came to realize is that with each trial, our heavenly Father was introducing himself to us in a more intimate way. Love was wooing us. Whether the experience resulted in a positive, negative, or neutral emotion, it was another facet of God's love toward us. And if we missed the revelation of who he was in the encounter, the lesson returned. Love was pursuing us. As you will see in the pages of this book, he wants us to know *at this moment* who we are, whose we are, and where we are in Christ.

I have witnessed Patricia's evolutionary and ongoing process of discovering who and whose she is and where she is in Christ. I can attest to her unwavering faith and belief that she is an eternal child of El Elyon (God Most High). I authenticate her position in Christ—increasing in the knowledge of God. I am the student recipient of the teacher that God has gifted to rightly divide his word. This book is a necessary balm during a climate of despair, spiritual apathy, and identity crisis. Since the fall of man (Adam) in the book of Genesis, God has poured out his love toward us. Sin separated us (Adam) from God, and he longed for us to be restored to him. In his unconditional love God sent his only begotten son to reconcile us to him.

Today, in this fallen world, we are still in need of a Savior's reconciliation. Sin and other distractions compete and win our time and love for God. We move away from God and find ourselves in emotional, physical, and financial distress. We look to our family members, doctors, banks, and even our president to rescue us, only to discover paucity. People don't need an insufficient, temporary bailout plan. People need the *Lord*!

Patricia directly, but inoffensively, challenges new and mature Christians alike through seven points to gain a greater knowledge of Christ in order that "thy will be done." Do you need to move closer to God to remember *who* and *whose* you are? Perhaps you are pondering where you are in Christ. I pray that as you read this book and participate in the focus and meditation scriptures at the beginning of each chapter, you will discover God afresh and anew and love him more. Get excited and read in expectation! You *will* experience a wonderful spiritual transformation.

—Cecelia L. Harris
Sisters4Life
Largo Community Church

Point One

What Love Is

For God so loved the world that he gave his only
begotten Son that whosoever believeth in him
should not perish but have everlasting life.

John 3:16 (KJV)

Saints, we are in the middle of a battle, but we war not
against flesh and blood. This fight cannot be fought
with physical hands, but by the mighty hand of God.
The enemy has been deceiving us in this area and
causing many casualties on our side for far too long.
We need to get the truth out, and that's where you

and I come in. The Bible is our offense, defense, and our final authority. If we apply it to our situations, circumstances, and to every area of our lives, change has to occur. The Word of God *is the final say*, and that *settles it*!

We find in this scripture that love is *giving*, love is *faithful*, love is *considerate*, and love is *rewarding*. *Love is giving* because God *gave* his Son as the ultimate sin offering for you and me. We would not exist had it not been for this awesome sacrifice. *Love is faithful* because God promised his people a Savior. Isaiah 9:6–7 (KJV) reads:

> For unto us a child is born, unto us a son is given: and the government shall be upon his shoulder: and his name shall be called Wonderful, Counsellor, The mighty God, The everlasting Father, The Prince of Peace. Of the increase of his government and peace there shall be no end, upon the throne of David, and upon his kingdom, to order it, and to establish it with judgment and with justice from henceforth even for ever. The zeal of the LORD of hosts will perform this.

The only thing required of us is that we believe in our hearts Jesus is who scripture say he is, God's Son, and that we confess this revelation or truth to all we come in contact with. Not only should this confession be done with words, but it should most assuredly be done through our lifestyles—our everyday living. Love is *considerate* because God cared so much for mankind that he devised a plan to save us from eternal damnation.

> The Lord is not slack concerning his promise, as some men count slackness; but is longsuffering to us-ward, not willing that any should perish, but that all should come to repentance.
>
> 2 Peter 3:9 (KJV)

And finally, love is *rewarding* because God promises his children the ultimate gift—eternal life. Eternal life is a gift or reward from God through Jesus Christ which enables us to live forever in his presence. Let's take a look at 1 Corinthians 15:49–53 (KJV).

> And as we have borne the image of the earthy, we shall also bear the image of the heavenly. Now this I say, brethren, that flesh and blood

cannot inherit the kingdom of God; neither doth corruption inherit incorruption. Behold, I shew you a mystery; We shall not all sleep, but we shall all be changed, In a moment, in the twinkling of an eye, at the last trump: for the trumpet shall sound, and the dead shall be raised incorruptible, and we shall be changed. For this corruptible must put on incorruption, and this mortal must put on immortality.

These passages of scripture are reminding us of our beginning and our ending. In the beginning, we were formed from the materials of this world, the dust of the ground. The body or flesh will return to where it came from, and likewise, our spirit will return to where it belongs. But in the end, we will be translated from mortality into immortality. What a glorious day that will be!

We've tried for so long showing up to this fight with physical weaponry. But now the truth is out, so let's cause some major damage to the enemy's camp. Let's increase our army by recruiting the broken hearted, the down trodden, and those who society have mistakenly kicked to the curb because they thought they would not amount to anything, let alone be a threat. Sound familiar? This may be you, and if so, God is looking for a few good men and women who will stand for righteousness' sake. Will you stand with us?

So where do we start? Well, with most things, you start at the beginning. First, you should know your Commander-in-chief. Most Christians believe God is untouchable, that he just sits on his throne and shows himself seasonally or on occasion. This is far from the truth. God is alive, and his spirit resides in each of his believers. God is all powerful and all knowing. God is merciful and giving. He has emotions. God is real! He's the one who placed the moon in the sky, and he's the creator of life. God is Alpha and Omega, the beginning and the ending of everything.

My question to you is do you know him personally as one of the above? You see, if you haven't experienced anything or been through something where you could honestly say, it had to be God that brought you out, you can't know him, not personally.

Believe it or not, many Christians miss this part. God desires a personal relationship with each one of his children; he has since the creation of Adam and Eve. Intimacy!

We were designed to *desire* intimacy with God.

Our lives were created for intimacy through companionship. But many of us begin to search for this intimacy in mere man, and each time we've been disappointed. We will never fulfill that void of perfect intimacy with man because man didn't place it within us. Until we renew a broken relationship with God through Christ Jesus, we will never be whole. Like I mentioned earlier, everything starts with a beginning, and our beginning starts with God. In the beginning, God created man for his very own pleasure. He created us to commune with him, which means we relate with him. This is possible only through a renewed spirit, acceptance and acknowledgement of Jesus Christ as Lord and Savior.

If someone were to ask you how you know God loves you, how would you answer them? Could you answer them in your own way and in your own words? Could you even put it into words? Would you base your answer(s) on unanswered prayer or results from a devastating event or circumstance that occurred in your life? Does your faith dictate to you that if God didn't do another thing for you, saving you from eternal damnation in hell and doing this through the shed blood of his Son Jesus would be more than enough to prove that he loves you?

God so loved the world that he gave his only begotten Son, that whosoever believes in him should not perish but have everlasting life (John 3:16 (KJV)). The scripture does not say God loved a certain group of people, but it states that God loved the world. Even in its worst state, he still loves the world. And it is his will that all believe in his Son Jesus unto salvation. There are some who say if that is true, then why won't he see to it that all believe since he has the power to do so? But the answer is simple. He is a God of love, and because he loves us, he has given us a free will. God did not intend for us to be robots but to freely give and show love.

In the Garden of Eden, God gave Adam and Eve an opportunity to choose good or evil, and he explained the consequence. You could say that God gave them an opportunity to show that they loved him more than anything or anyone else. They failed to do so. Rather, they proved that we are a selfish people and we continue to allow things and people to separate us from God's love. Today there's no difference; God continues to allow us to act from our own freewill or freedom of choice. In acting according to our own free will, God has been calling us since the beginning of time to be obedient to his Word. But over the ages, we've continued to fall short in this area, and we displease God.

Webster's tells us love is "an unselfish, loyal, and benevolent concern for the good of another, as the fatherly concern for mankind." *Webster's* was on to something when it penned the definition for love. The key to any successful relationship is love. Love, when it is the principle ingredient, brings about a certain level of commitment to a relationship. God has always held up his end concerning love for his children.

God's love has no end. If we would just dare to imagine what he gave up to prove his love for us, maybe we would begin to cherish, respect, and honor the love he has for us. The truth is, he wrapped himself in flesh (God and Jesus are one) and allowed his Son to be beaten to within inches of death, sentenced to die by crucifixion, and above all of that, was predestined to take on *all* of the sins of the world. God did that for you and me. He loves us enough to give us an opportunity to live with him in heaven for an eternity. Now that's love! And all he asks in return is that we love him with everything within us and that we love all people as ourselves. God wants us to live in peace and harmony with one another. It is his will that none perish. We know that everyone won't accept Christ, but nevertheless, it is God's will that they would. If we don't show compassion to those people deemed unlovable, how can we say we know him who is full of compassion? If we don't have patience with those in need, how can we say we know him who has been patient with us? If we don't display love to those we come in contact with, we can't say we know the one who is love. I know these are some tough truths, but we must ponder them to know where we are in Christ. We can only move forward once we recognize where we are and where we've been. It is imperative that we portray Christ in our daily living. After all, the Holy Spirit does dwell within every believer and equips us to be able to do just that; live for Christ. We were saved for a purpose, and we were saved with a purpose.

Our relationship with God is the most important relationship we can and will ever have. In the beginning, God created us in his image and in their likeness (Genesis 2). We are a triune being, made up of three parts, which consists of a spirit, a soul, and a body. It is our spirit man that gets renewed once we accept Jesus. But prior to acceptance of Christ, we were in darkness, separated from our Creator, because of the fall of man in the Garden of Eden. Because of Adam and Eve's disobedience, we were all born into sin and shaped in iniquity. It took the blood of an unblemished lamb (one who did not know nor commit sin) to atone for the sins of the world. That sacrificial lamb was Jesus.

"And I give unto them eternal life; and they shall never perish, neither shall any man pluck them out of my hand" (John 10:28 (KJV)). What exactly do we gain when we accept God's Son Jesus, who gave himself as a ransom for our transgression, as Lord and Savior? We gain the opportunity to reign with Jesus in the presence of God for an eternity in heaven. The flip side of that is living eternally in hell with the devil and being tormented for ever. You see, God's children (those who except Christ) will never perish but will continue to live life in abundance. The scripture goes on to say that neither shall any man pluck us out of the hand of Jesus. I'm sorry, but I wouldn't want to serve a God who was incapable of keeping me, just as he has said, until the day of redemption. That's the kind of God we worship. One that is all-powerful, all-knowing, and full of love. I may be opening up a can of worms, but that's all right. If you caught a hold of what I just said, you'll know and believe that once saved, you are always saved. I know some people dispute this fact, but the truth is in the Word of God. If you are saved, and only God knows the answer to that, you should be fully persuaded that nothing can or will separate you from the love of God, which is in and through Jesus Christ. We tend to sit on the seat of judgment and pretty much do Jesus' job for him. Only God is omniscient (all-knowing), and only he knows the end of a thing. I'm sure there are a number of people who we believed would not amount to anything and we may have written them off, but that's exactly who God will reach down for, dust off, and set them up to be a blessing to every doubter known and unknown. Don't think for a moment that during your life there weren't any pharaohs (people or things that oppress) in your life. We all had them or currently have them. They are there to prove that our God cares for us and that he is still in control and in the miracle-working business. His main objective is to show himself through the believer, so that the nonbeliever can change and turn from the world's way and turn back to God. I often share with others that haven't surrendered their lives to Christ that there is a misconception about accepting God's salvation. This misconception is partly blamed due to the church, the saints. We've led people to believe that you must be holy to be saved, when it's quite the contrary. We must be saved to become holy. So nonbelievers alike are turned away, believing that they must give up all the things the world says are cool; things like smoking cigarettes or weed, pre-marital sex, drinking, and other things that do not meet with God's approval. When you really think about it, these things destroy the body. And let's not forget the things that not only affect the body but affect the heart or spirit as well. Things like lying, gossiping, complaining, and envying. But my Bible tells me that I can come just as I am. I can come with all my issues, be it issues of the heart, flesh, or spirit. Once we accept Christ, we gain the Holy Spirit, who then takes up residence within us to help us live righteously unto God. It is the Holy Spirit's responsibility to help us turn from those things that are not pleasing to God. When we attempt to do those things, we will be prompted, and it will be made known that we shouldn't do that. Now there will be instances where we will override the Holy Spirit and do it anyway. In those cases, we need to ask forgiveness and try our best to turn from doing those things. The turning away is called repenting! We'll get into that a little later.

Just be mindful that it is the Holy Spirit who gives us the power to be obedient to the will of God. If we had the power to change, we would have done it a long time ago; I know I would have. You see, I haven't been living for Jesus all of my life. I began seeking for more, or rather seeking a relationship with God, at age twenty-nine. I was going to Mass on Sundays (or Saturday's at 5:00 p.m. if I planned to hang out all night on Saturday), and one particular Sunday morning, I recall sitting in service and thinking to myself, *There's gotta be more to this than just sitting here Sunday after Sunday.*

Little did I know God was beginning to woo me back to him. At this point, I began to search and find truth (Jesus is the truth, the way, and the life). I have been seeking after him ever since. Has my walk been squeaky clean? *No.* The Bible tells us in Romans 3:23 that *all have sinned, and come short of the glory of God.* This is another misconception, that when you began to live your life for Christ's sake, everything will be peaches and cream, not so. God has to test and perfect that which is in you, and sometimes we fail the test, but we try again! This is why it is important to be yoked to a Bible-teaching, Word-living church.

Point Two

What Love Made You

Wherefore come out from among them, and
be ye separate, saith the Lord, and touch not
the unclean thing; and I will receive you.

2 Corinthians 6:17 (KJV)

In order for us to have a successful relationship
with God, a separation and cleansing must take
place. Notice that the words *separation* and *cleansing*
are joined together by the conjunction *and*. In this
instance, its purpose (the conjunction) is to be as one
thought and not to stand alone. In other words you

can't do one without doing the other. The reason separation and cleansing are very vital in our relationship to God is first, it allows us to take off our old nature, and secondly, it enables us to be in the presence of our heavenly Father. Our old nature cannot be in the presence of God without being destroyed (Isaiah 39:2). Sin not only separates us from God, but it also hides his face from us.

When we look at the birthing process of a woman, we find that the baby, who has been connected to the mother via the umbilical cord, has access to the mother's nutrients. At the time of birth, there comes a time of separation where the baby gets disconnected from the mother. Once this happens, the baby is then taken away from the mother for a few moments to be cleansed. Before the separation, the baby was dependent upon the mother and accustomed to the way things flowed to it from its mother. Before we accept Christ, we too are accustomed to the way the world acts and reacts, thereby, adjusting and accepting what it does as the norm for our lives. When the time presents itself for us to be in right relationship with God, or to be reconciled back to him, we accept his gift of eternal life made available through his Son

Jesus Christ. It is at that time that we begin to live life in obedience to God's holy Word. This is not an easy transition, but it is a necessary one. This is not something that will happen overnight, rather it's something that takes a lifetime to actually perfect.

In trying to attempt perfection through the blood of Jesus, we must know our worth. We were fearfully and wonderfully made! We were made for God's pleasure and for his glory. Validation for us only comes from God. If this is true, why do we "people please?" Why do we look to man to tell us what we are worth? The truth is we haven't accepted what the Word of God says about us. We can't grasp the truth that we were, in fact, fearfully and wonderfully made by God, because *we* are different from the majority or those who society deems as the norm. We can't stand being different, being the "called out," so what do we do? We try to fit in. Saints, it won't work! You were made for God's purpose. He has designed a life for you that will cause you to make ripples in the lives of the people you come in contact with. He has devised a plan that will incorporate healing, deliverance, and salvation for all who will accept his Son, and you are the vessel he wants to use to carry this ministry of reconciliation to the masses (Matthew 28:18–20). So you see, you can't be like them (the world) because they need to see the work in progress of what they are about to take part and participate in. They need to see that the God you and I serve does make a difference in the lives of his children. They need to know beyond a shadow of doubt that *God is real* and he is who you say he is! They need to know that he rewards those who diligently seek after him. The key word is *seek*. The word *seek* is a verb which, in this instance, means to try to find. Keep in mind, we're not seeking to find God because he's not lost, we are; but we seek after him to find his attributes and his characteristics. When we come to know these things, we can then know God in the way he intended us to know him, intimately. Yes, we were made in his image and in their likeness, but the characteristics of Jesus we must obtain through Christian maturity, better known as the three Ts: test, trial, and tribulation (Romans 5:3–6).

> And not only so, but we glory in tribulations also: knowing that tribulation worketh patience; And patience, experience; and experience, hope: And hope maketh not ashamed; abroad in our

hearts by the Holy Ghost which is given unto us. For when we were yet without strength, in due time Christ died for the ungodly.

Romans 5:3–6 (KJV)

We'll get into the three Ts and what is meant by Christian maturity in Point Three. Let me begin, though, by saying without faith it is impossible to please (do anything for) God (Hebrews 11:6). Faith is the key! Faith is the key that gives us access to God and all his promises. The Bible states no one can come unto the Father (God) except by him (Jesus) (John 14:16). Without belief in Jesus Christ, access is denied to come unto the Father. We must believe that Jesus is the Son of God, that he died, was buried, and that God did raise him from the dead. This belief in Christ automatically gives us access to the Father, saves us from the penalty of sin, which is eternal damnation, and gives us an opportunity to reign with Jesus in heaven. When we accept Christ's plan of salvation for our lives, we've fulfilled the prerequisite for becoming a child of God or a Christian (to be Christlike).

When we really think about it, the first step, though it may have taken many of us some time to truly submit to, was actually an easy step to take. We know that God is Creator, and if he can create a world from nothing except the spoken word and create everything in it, why couldn't he resurrect (give life to again) his Son Jesus? Why would it be difficult for us to believe (have faith, trust)? You see, our entire relationship with God is based upon faith. All the promises listed in the Bible that are from God are predicated upon our faith and our obedience.

"Now faith is the substance of things hoped for, the evidence of things not seen" (Hebrews 11:1 (KJV)). My personal interpretation of this scripture is faith is the reality of a promise given by God that we know will come to pass because we know he's good on his word. Keep in mind, faith isn't something that happens overnight, the maturing that is. It is liken unto a seed. St. Matthew correlates faith to a mustard seed (Matthew 17:20). Anytime you water a seed that has germinated properly, it is destined to grow. Unlike the mustard seed, our faith doesn't need watering. On the contrary, that's the problem with most of us now, we possess watered-down faith. Our faith requires the three Ts to increase and mature.

Now that we have a basic understanding of

Christian maturity and faith, our spirit should be open to accept and understand the three Ts (test, trial, and tribulation).

- *Test*—a critical examination, observation, or evaluation; a basis for evaluation
- *Trial*—the action or process of trying or putting to the proof; test; a test of faith, patience, or stamina by suffering or temptation
- *Tribulation*—distress or suffering from oppression or persecution; also a trying experience

To further understand and accept the tests and trials we encounter, we must comprehend its purpose. The first purpose of a test or trial is to *measure our faith.* Keep in mind that God always knows the outcome of every test and trial we encounter, therefore, the burden of proof lies with us. We can say we will do thus and so and in all actuality do something totally contrary to what we thought we would do. The test or trial is an event that allows us to see where we *really* are in Christ. Romans 12:2 reminds us that we were all given a measure of faith, and even with that measure, we are not to think highly of ourselves but rather remembering Christ, the gift giver and the purpose he has placed in each of us. The second purpose of a test or trial is to *help someone else get through his or her trial.* I'm sure we've all heard the saying "it's not about you, but it's always about Christ." This is a true statement even during the storms of life, when we feel all hope is lost and there's no relief in sight, those times when it appears that everything that could go wrong, did go wrong. And those times when we get to a place in our lives where we question whether God is still with us and that he knowingly allows these things to go astray in our lives. Yes, this is a time of tribulation, a time of testing, pruning, and refining. This should be a time of joy. But it seldom is because we don't quite fully understand what is happening to us, nor do we know why. Often times we may never know the latter, but we do know that *all* things, both the good and the bad, will work together for our good (Romans 8:28). What happens to us is that we are deemed ready by God to suffer persecution at the hand of the enemy for Christ's sake. I pray that you caught that and if you did, you should be getting your shout on right about now! Let's take a look at the book of Job 1:6–8 (KJV).

Now there was a day when the sons of God came to present themselves before the LORD, and Satan came also among them. And the LORD said unto Satan, Whence comest thou? Then Satan answered the LORD, and said, From going to and fro in the earth, and from walking up and down in it. And the LORD said unto Satan, Hast thou considered my servant Job, that there is none like him in the earth, a perfect and an upright man, one that feareth God, and escheweth evil?

Here we see that because of Job's relationship and his right standing with God, God has granted Satan permission to test him. During the meeting which took place in heaven between God and the sons of God (angels), Satan showed up. The purpose of Satan's tour on earth was to see who he could torment and cause to fall. Since God knew Job was a perfect and upright man and he knew Job's heart, he offered Job to be tested. God knows *all* things. God knows what will cause us to fall, and he knows what will make us turn away from him and curse him. There are going to be times in your walk as a child of God where you will be tested. The tests are not meant to hurt you, rather to mold your character into Christlike character.

Job had a very hard test. I'm not sure if any of us could handle such a hard, traumatic test, but be very clear, *God knows.* And he will never put more on anyone than what they are able to bear. Again, God is Alpha and Omega, the beginning and the end, so he knows well in advance what we can handle and what we cannot handle. We must remember when we are being tested, if the test is from God, he has already equipped us and given us what we need to pass it. What we really need to do is to trust him more and allow him to do his job, and that is to be *God!*

God's Word must be tested. Psalms 18:30 (KJV) tells us, "As for God, his way is perfect: the word of the LORD is tried: he is a buckler to all those that trust in him." We also find in Psalms 12:6 (KJV) that "the words of the LORD's are pure words: as silver tried in a furnace of earth, purified seven times." If you have any word hidden in your heart, that word must be tested.

In the book of Matthew 4:1–11 it records the temptation of Jesus. He was tested in three areas. He was tempted regarding his immediate need; his substance (verses 2–4). He was tempted regarding his relationship, his position in God (verses 6–9). And finally, he was tempted regarding his eternal identity, who he worshipped (verses 8–10).

Those of us who have accepted Christ as Lord and Savior carry the Word within us; therefore, we too, just as Christ, must be tempted and tried as a result of the Word we know. The word *know* means to understand from experience or attainment. In this usage, *know* means being intimate and having an understanding about the subject, not just reciting from memory. When we know something, we are aware of its truths and can relate to it due to personal experience. When we know God's Word intimately, we begin to know God intimately. Do you know him today?

The Word wrapped in flesh was led into the wilderness by the Holy Spirit to be tempted of the devil (Matthew 4:1). God will only test us on the Word we already know. It would not be fair if he tried us on something we haven't understood or learned yet. But God knows if we learned a thing, even if *we* don't realize we've already learned it. You see, tests aren't to let God know that we can pass them; he is omniscient, he knows everything. On the contrary, the outcome is for us to realize where we are in our Christian walk. Always remember, if you don't pass the test the first time, it will be coming back around again (Ecclesiastes 3:15), but it may be a little more difficult than the first time.

As we look at the text written in Matthew chapter 4, we recognize that the areas the enemy will come after us are:

- our immediate needs
- our relationship with God
- our eternal identity

Our Immediate Need (Matthew 4:1–4)

In Matthew 4:2, the Bible says Jesus had been fasting for forty days and nights. Fasting is neglecting the body of food and/or drink for a specific time and purpose. This let's me know Jesus was hungry. Our immediate needs include, but are not limited to, food, clothing, finances, etc.

All our trials, tribulations, and temptations are not a result of disobedience, but some are strategically put into play to get us moving into the right direction, God's direction for our lives. Therefore, every time something goes wrong in our lives, we shouldn't ask, "What did I do to deserve this?" instead we should be asking, "What would you like for me to learn from this?" Now let's look at what Jesus did to combat the enemy's attack. Verse four says "man shall not live by bread alone, but by every word that proceeds out of the mouth of God." The natural food supplies the body, and the Word of God supplies our spirit man. Just as the natural body needs food to survive, likewise, our spirit man needs *its* food to survive. In Deuteronomy 8:2–3, God led his people (the Israelites) into the wilderness to humble them, to test them and to let them know what was in their hearts. He allowed them to be hungry so they would learn to depend and trust in him to provide their immediate need, which in that particular instance was food. And he fed them with manna from on high.

God gave us his Word because it is profitable for doctrine, reproof, correction, and instruction, that we may be perfect and thoroughly furnished unto all good works (2 Timothy 3:16–17). Know that we will never attain perfection on this side, but what the scripture is suggesting is that we strive for perfection in righteousness through Jesus Christ.

Our Relationship with God (Matthew 4:5–7)

Notice here in our text where Jesus is being tempted a second time, we see something very interesting. We see the devil reciting the Word of God. Our relationship with God should be based on one thing, faith. First Peter 1:3–9 (KJV) says:

> Blessed be the God and Father of our Lord Jesus Christ, which according to his abundant mercy hath begotten us again unto a lively hope by the resurrection of Jesus Christ from the dead. To an inheritance incorruptible, and undefiled, and that fadeth not away, reserved in heaven for you, Who are kept by the power of God through faith unto salvation ready to be revealed in the last time. Wherein ye greatly rejoice, though now for a season, if need be, ye are in heaviness through manifold temptations: That the trial of your faith, being much more precious than of gold that perisheth, though it be tried with fire, might be found unto praise and honour and glory at the appearing of Jesus Christ: Whom having not seen, ye love; in whom, though now ye see him not, yet believing, ye rejoice with joy un-

speakable and full of glory: Receiving the end
of your faith, even the salvation of your souls.

Without faith, it is impossible to please God. It is by
faith that we all are justified (Acts 13:39, paraphrased).
Notice I said the devil recited the Word of God. The
difference with him and us is that we are to have faith
in the Word (the Word wrapped in flesh as well as the
logos, written Word). Our relationship with God is
feasible through faith and in our prayers. It is by faith
we believe unto salvation, and it's through prayer that
we communicate or commune with him. Once we are
reconnected to God, through the sacrifice of Jesus,
nothing should separate us from him.

The enemy in verse five is suggesting to Christ,
"If you are who you say you are, then prove it to me."
How many of you have been in this predicament,
being faced with a battle that's not yours to fight, but
the enemy is egging you on to respond? Whenever
you're faced with this dilemma, just remember, the
battle belongs to the Lord (2 Chronicles 20:15). If you
open your mouth on his behalf, he will give you the
words to say. Jesus' response to Satan was, "Thou shalt
not tempt the Lord thy God." Again, here's where

faith comes into play. When we believe God at his Word, there is no need to try to trick or tempt him into doing anything for us.

Our Eternal Identity (Matthew 4:8–10)

The third temptation found in Matthew chapter four attacks our eternal identity. Will we choose God and make heaven our eternal home, or will we choose Satan and make hell our eternal resting place? The choice is left to us. In verse nine, the enemy promises to give Christ the world if he would only bow down to worship him. I would like to make this as plain and simple as I possibly can. Knowing where Christ came from, did he really want *this* world? I think not. Christ didn't want it, and God instructs us in 1 John 2:15–16 (KJV) to "Love not the world, neither the things that are in the world. If any man love the world, the love of the Father is not in him. For all that is in the world, the lust of the flesh, and the lust of the eyes, and the pride of life, is not of the Father, but is of the world." Satan is the prince of the world. Who or what we continue to serve will determine our eternal identity.

Point Three

The Kingdom of God

And they overcame him by the blood of the
Lamb, and by the word of their testimony;
and they loved not their lives unto the death.

Revelation 12:11 (KJV)

We know now who we are and whose we are. We also
know that because we bare the name of Christ Jesus,
we, too, will be persecuted, but we are not forsaken.
We understand that during this walk we will be tested
and during our test we are to count it all joy because it
is working together for our good. We've laid the basic

foundation, and now we can build upon that and proceed to the meat of the matter. How do we become a citizen of the kingdom of God?

First, we must comprehend what the phrase the kingdom of God means. *Kingdom,* according to *Webster's Dictionary,* is the external kingship of God; the realm in which God's will is fulfilled. That just blew my natural mind! God's kingdom is wherever his will is being fulfilled. We know that God resides in eternity. We also know that he is as close to us as our next breath. God is in all places at the same time. But we need to understand that where his will is being fulfilled, there he is too, in his fullness. God has a permissive will as well as a perfect will, the latter being way more important and necessary. In God's permissive will, he permits us to have some of the things we want or think we need. But the safest place to be is in God's perfect will. In God's perfect will, we walk in total obedience to his will for our lives and we are able to reap the benefits thereof. When we look at what transpired with Abram and Sari, we see this principle in action.

God promised Abram he would be a great nation (Genesis 12:2) and he would make Abram's seed as the dust of the earth (Genesis 13:16). This would mean

Abram would have to father children in order for this to come to pass. But Sarai, who was barren (Genesis 11:30), demonstrated absolutely no faith that God would or could allow her to conceive. You see, like Sarai, we get caught up in the natural and we miss the possibilities of the supernatural. But yet again, God confirmed his promise to Abram about the vast number of his offspring or seed by equating them to the endless number of stars in the heavens (Genesis 15:5). At this time, Abram was ready for the promise to be fulfilled because he asked God in Genesis 15:2, (KJV) "What will you give me, seeing I go childless?" I suppose Sarai grew a little weary as well, because her next move proved to be a move of desperation on her part. In Genesis 16:2–3, Sarai suggests to Abram that he go in to her handmaid, Hagar, so that she can bare him the child of promise. Now ladies, when you know your husband has sho 'nough heard from the Lord regarding a promise and he has given him (your husband) specific instructions, don't try to add your two cents to it, because you just may be causing more mess than is necessary. This goes out to the husbands as well.

Many of us know the outcome of this story, but to show how vitally important it is to be obedient to

God's will and plan for our lives, let's see how the story ended. Sarai's handmaid did conceive and birthed a male child, and they named him Ishmael. Please keep in mind what looks like a blessing may not be the blessing at all, but rather it can be God's permissive will in action. We, like Sarai, have problems with waiting. When we do not wait, we show God two things: first, we show him we do not believe or trust him, and second, we show him we have a better plan or a better way of doing it. Waiting requires patience and patience requires work. Allow me to explain exactly what I mean. Exhibiting patience shows that you are *resting in the truth*. It also proves you are confident in the promise coming to pass. Now, the work portion shows forth the evidence of patience. One of my memorable scriptures states that faith without works is dead (James 2:17). Because Sarai looked at the *facts*, which showed that she was too old to conceive and carry a baby full term, she missed the *truth* that God specializes in things that seem impossible. Sarai saw no other way due to her lack of faith. Faith expands what the eyes cannot see.

God has promised many of us a few things that we are unable to do in our own strength, but the purpose of his plan is designed to teach us not to rely on self but rather to trust whole heartedly in him. There is no failure in God. I know there's a great number of us waiting on the manifestation of the things God has promised us, and I say this to you and to myself, hold on to exactly what God has told you and do not lose hope. Do not lose your focus, and always remember that all of God's promises are yeah and amen! Abram was told again that his wife Sarah would conceive and the child's name shall be Isaac. At this point in Abraham's life, he too had a hard time believing Sarah, at an old age, could bare a child.

As the account of Abraham and Sarah proceeds, we find that Sarah did in fact bare Abraham a son and his name was Isaac, just as God had commanded. This, my brothers and sisters, was God's perfect will for Abraham and Sarah. Yes, there was a *blessing* attached to Ishmael coming on the scene, but God had *covenant* with Isaac. Genesis 17:20–21 (KJV):

> And as for Ishmael, I have heard thee: Behold, I have blessed him, and will make him fruitful, and will multiply him exceedingly; twelve princes shall he beget, and I will make him a

great nation. But my covenant will I establish
with Isaac, which Sarah shall bear unto thee at
this set time in the next year.

Always choose to be in God's perfect will and you shall
experience covenant relationship with El Shaddai,
God Almighty.

Is God's kingdom present in you? Do people know
that there's a safe haven in coming to you for Godly
wisdom and advice? When you are a citizen of God's
kingdom, you must exhibit some of his characteristics. Another thing that should be evident is our faith.
Without faith, it is impossible to please God.

Becoming a citizen of the kingdom of God has
a two-fold criterion. First, you must be born again.
You must except Christ as Lord and Savior and be
obedient to God's statutes, rules, and command-
ments. Secondly, you must have evidence that you
are a citizen. I'm sure you're wondering how this is
done. Well, as it was stated in the paragraph above,
God's will should be fulfilled or begin to be fulfilled in
your life. This is not an easy task to accomplish. Once
the enemy sees you're making great strides to fulfill
God's will and purpose in your life, he will attempt to

discredit you with your past, shortcomings, and failures. But this is where the privileges of being a citizen in the kingdom of God pays off. God promises his children that no weapon formed against them shall prosper. The weapons will be formed, but they cannot prosper in the area the enemy intends harm.

For so long we have believed that we were in a fight, and during those times, we believed it was our fight to fight. And in our train of thought, we advanced accordingly, and every time we did, we were handed a defeat. Know that this fight is not between us and Satan. No, this fight is between God and Satan. We are just innocent or not-so-innocent bystanders. We are in the middle, and there's only one thing God has asked us to do during this fight. *Stand!* We are asked to stand fast in faith (1 Corinthians 16:13). We are asked to stand fast in one spirit (Philippians 1:27). And we are also asked to stand fast in the Lord (Philippians 4:1).

Since the days of John the Baptist until now, the kingdom of heaven suffereth violence, and the violent take it by force (Matthew 11:12). The kingdom of God has been under attack since the days of John the Baptist and even now.

If you are a child of God, you should be receiving

opposition in some area of your life, simply because you belong to Christ. But to suffer for and with Christ is gain! It is time we as believers take our position as joint heirs with Christ and show this dying world who we really are and what our God is really capable of doing. We must get fired up in our spirit to the point where we are fulfilling the will of our heavenly Father and not the lusts of our flesh. There should be a distinction between a believer and a nonbeliever. Our witness to others should always line up with God's Holy Word. It's time we get radical in the things of God and put away those things that only matter to our flesh. We should esteem our brothers and sisters above ourselves and not try to outdo them due to selfish pride. We need to encourage rather than tear down, to lend a helping hand instead of asking for a handout. Let's get out of self and into Christ, who not only cared for you and me, but gave his life so that we can escape God's wrath.

Much of this book is pure repetition. And it is obvious that we are a people who need to hear repeatedly in order for change to occur. The Bible tells us that we are overcomers because Christ overcame the world. Our lead scripture is reemphasizing that we have already overcome the enemy because of Jesus' bloodshed and, in addition to that, our testimonies play a role in this as well. When we remember what God has previously brought us out of and we share that information with others, we are giving that person strength to stand during the fight and a hope that they, too, have already won. Our testimonies also help us gird up for the next trial, as we remember how God got us through the last trial.

Listen, once we get on one accord with truly knowing and living God's Word, the things of this world will not matter as much. Our lead scripture ends by saying "and they loved not *their* lives unto the death." Who does this remind you of? Jesus! He specifically came to die. We, too, were born to die to our fleshly nature. It is the worldly things that distract us from being godly disciples. Where there is an earthly connection, there is a foot hole for Satan to tempt us. When we have heavenly connections, he has no dominion or power there. Jesus told the disciples in Luke 14:26, (KJV) "If any man come to me, and hate not his father, and mother, and wife, and children, and brethren, and sisters, yea, and his own life also, he cannot be my disciple." Learn to lay down your life and take up the life God has prepared for you.

Point Four

Thy Kingdom Come

> After this manner pray ye: Our Father which art in heaven, Hallowed be thy name. Thy kingdom come. Thy will be done in earth, as it is in heaven.
>
> Matthew 6:9–10 (KJV)

In a kingdom, there's one ruler, and the ruler of that kingdom makes the rules or decrees for that kingdom. Those who choose and are chosen to be a part of this kingdom must obey the rules or decrees set by the king or ruler. The decrees are never to be altered in any way by the inhabitants of the kingdom—only the king or ruler can change or alter a decree that has been set. A kingdom is built and prepared by the king or ruler for its inhabitants. Our kingdom (God's kingdom) is ruled by God; God is our supreme and solemn ruler. The rules that have been set by God are outlined in scripture and can be found in the Holy Bible. It is through prayer that the scriptures and decrees are mouthed so that God's rules can be manifested here on earth.

This is why when we pray, "Thy kingdom come, thy will be done in earth as it is in heaven," we are asking God to allow his reign-ship or rule to have dominion in us (the called) here on earth. When we pray "thy kingdom come," we are asking God to disburse the order of heaven into our earthen vessels. When we pray "thy will be done," we give God permission to orchestrate our lives according to his plans. When we pray "thy will be done," we release probabilities which turn into possibilities. When we pray "thy will be done," we release the mind of Christ into this earth realm which produces God's kingdom right here on earth.

Once we have grasped hold of the power that lies within this very powerful verse of scripture, we will begin to become *kingdom minded*, which will in turn produce kinship or citizens of the kingdom of God. When we become full-fledged citizens of God's kingdom, the atmosphere on this side will begin to shift. Shifting is possible only through the Holy Spirit. God anoints us to perform his plan in this earth realm. God promised us he would pour out his spirit upon all flesh (Joel 2:28, Acts 2:17). Children of God, that time is now!

God is not a man that he can tell a lie. Whatever he says, it shall come to pass. His promises are always yea and amen. But there are levels to the anointing of God, and these levels are something we are to seek after. We are reminded in Hebrews 11:6 that he rewards those who diligently seek Him. There is no written formula to systematically ascertain a new level in Christ Jesus. This is solely God's decision as to who receives how much anointing and when they should receive each level. Our job is to seek the face of the One who holds and disperses the anointing. We were instructed in Matthew 6:33 to seek first the kingdom of God and all its righteousness and everything else we will ever need will be given to us (paraphrase). There is something very important in seeking. To seek after something means you are earnestly looking with zeal and with expectation to find what it is you are seeking. When we seek after something, we are not satisfied until we find it. I pray you caught that!

What exactly are we seeking when we seek "the kingdom of God" or "thy will be done"? We're seeking the very thing that will change the inner man; the very thing that will cause us to conform to the image of Christ Jesus. We seek God's face and not what he can give us or do for us. We, as mature Christians, should no longer be seeking after a sugar daddy in our heavenly Father, but rather seeking to know his heart, his will, and his ways. We know we have matured when our prayers are no longer about our natural needs. We know we've matured when our prayers are no longer about ourselves. And we have most certainly matured when our prayer life goes from praying about things to praying about others. This, my brothers and sisters, is called intercession. I believe God is calling the body of Christ to a place of intercession. We often look at intercession as being one sided, but it is quite the contrary. Intercession begins being about someone else, but what it does is place you in a position to be ushered into God's presence, and after that, it becomes about you and God. In this place, you don't have to say a word, because God is doing all of the work. He begins to show us the deep things inside of us, and as he's doing that, things begin to fall off and we begin to look more and more like Jesus. What an awesome experience. But sadly, many Christians haven't even experienced a small portion of that, let alone, been taught how to enter God's presence and go beyond the veil. It is in this place that we are ministered to by our heavenly Father. But we are so concerned nowadays with seat filling that we've forgotten about the soul that's already sitting there that is in dire need of deliverance.

Let's cast our anchor here for a minute or so. I am not just talking about the pastor, but the lay members as well. There are saints who have been occupying the same seat for over twenty years and sitting back getting fat off of the Word of God. One would think that after such a long time you would have gained some discernment and begin to pray and intercede for your neighbor sitting on your pew or be able to disciple the new converts recently joining the church. This is not the case. We are so set on getting to church, finding our *same* seat, and hearing a Word for ourselves that we neglect to remember our neighbors, who Jesus has instructed us to love and care after. We have inundated ourselves with programs, fish fries and the like, year after year and never really bothered to see if this is what God wants us to do. So we plan just because we did it last year. All of these things have their place, but is it really what God would have us to do. Tradition, in the right place, is good, but out of context and the will of God, it can be harmful, prejudice, and hindering. Is that really being led by the Spirit? Saints, it's time for a change, a change in habit, a change in character, and definitely a change in our prayer life. People are experiencing real life issues, and we are overlooking them and brushing them under the carpet just so we can top last year's funding. Is God really pleased with this?

When Jesus calls his kingdom, it will take place in a twinkling of an eye. But the question remains, will we be ready to reign with Jesus in the New Jerusalem? I know you've heard it before, but the fact still remains, we are still in desperate need of a risen Savior to present us faultless before God. When will we begin to do what God has ordained us to do? When will we begin to know and recognize the differences between Jesus' rule and this world's system? Jeremiah 8:20 (KJV) says, "The harvest is past, the summer is ended, and we are not saved."

We continue to exhibit the same issues that were prevalent during the early church, which is, division. We insist upon dividing the Church into many different sects, and why? Because we fail to make it be about Christ and we continue to make it be about us. We are a selfish, faithless, and perverse generation. Church, we must prepare ourselves for the bridegroom. Has anyone ever wondered why Christ has not returned yet? It's simple—we're not ready!

Let's take a quick look at the book of Nehemiah. This book is filled with many jewels, and we could see them if we would just open our eyes of understanding and be enlightened. First, *Nehemiah had a heart towards God's people.* In chapter one, we find him inquiring about the Jews, which were left of the captivity (verse 2). The response from his peers about his inquisition was that the remnant that were left of the captivity *were in* great affliction and reproach (verse 3). How many of us know that even today the remnant of God suffers great affliction and criticism? Secondly, we see *Nehemiah had genuine concern for the welfare of God's chosen people.* And thirdly, *Nehemiah knew the ingredients for change; he wept, mourned, fasted, and prayed before the God of heaven* (verse 4).

Nehemiah felt compelled to seek godly counsel concerning God's people, so he prayed unto God. Who among us is more qualified than God to handle issues concerning His people? Nehemiah didn't want to run in there all willy-nilly and make more of a mess than was already present, so he consulted the One who has all knowledge concerning all things. Nehemiah consulted God. How often do you consult God concerning the cares of this world and even the things that are not of this world? And how often do you consult God only when you appear to be in a bind? If we would just turn to him daily to know his plan for our lives, how many mistakes would we avoid? Practice seeking God's wisdom with everything that concerns you, even the things you think may be miniscule to him. I consult God often about things that others may believe are unnecessary to bother God about. I make my request known unto him, and he answers. There's nothing neither too small nor too astronomical that God won't be concerned with if it has to do with you. The Bible teaches us that we have not because we ask not (James 4:2). God tells us to cast our cares upon him and he will give us rest (Matthew 11:28). Maybe some of us are tired because we haven't given everything over to God.

Nehemiah wept and mourned. Weeping and mourning in the Bible usually got God's attention. This shows that Nehemiah had compassion for God's people and for God's plan for the lives of his people. Weeping and mourning also portray a level of humility. When we humble ourselves before the King, we are entreating him to have full Lordship over our situations, circumstances, and every area of our lives. Humility gives God permission to have free course in our lives, and it notifies Him that we have stepped away from the issue because we fully trust him to bring us through.

The Bible says that Nehemiah fasted. When our minds are bombarded with thoughts that can easily stress us out or cause us to get off focus, we need a reprieve or a way to clear our minds of the clutter. Fasting is an excellent way to do just that and to get closer to God so that we can hear him clearer. Many interchange fasting with dieting. These are two totally different ideals. One has to do with the physical body (dieting) and the other has to do with the spirit of man (fasting). Fasting is simply abstaining from food and/or drink for a specified period of time. There are several different types of fasts, and many of them are found in the Bible.

Looking at the task set before Nehemiah, it is obvious that the task had to do with more than just rebuilding of the wall. In fact, it had a lot to do with rebuilding and restoring. First, rebuilding the relationship with God and also rebuilding the relationships around us. We can glean a lot from Nehemiah. God used Nehemiah to rebuild and restore both God's people and his kingdom. God has placed in his children the ministry of reconciliation and is calling us to help rebuild and restore others to their rightful position in him. Are you making yourself available to help reconcile others just as someone has helped to reconcile you?

Point Five

A Life of Compassion

For even hereunto were ye called: because Christ also suffered for us, leaving us an example, that we should follow his steps: Who did no sin, neither was guile found in his mouth: Who, when he was reviled, reviled not again; when he suffered, he threatened not; but committed himself to him that judgeth righteously: Who his own self bare our sins in his own body on the tree, that we, being dead to sins, should live unto righteousness: by whose stripes ye were healed. For ye were

> as sheep going astray; but are now returned
> unto the Shepherd and Bishop of your souls.
> 1 Peter 2:21–25 (KJV)

God has people in our lives for many reasons, and the reasons are very specific. Many of us who profess Christianity could use an extra dose of compassion for our fellow brothers and sisters in Christ, as well as the unsaved. How many of us have a friend or loved one who is married, engaged, or dating someone we didn't or don't approve of? I believe the majority of us have judged others in this scenario and/or we ourselves are that friend and have been judged. Come on, let's be real. We've mouthed those infamous words, "Why is she with him?" or "What made him marry her?" There are always three sides to a story: his version, her version, and then the truth, which is God's version. At any rate, we're going to take a look at two sides of this story.

As I stated earlier, God strategically allows certain people to enter our lives at specific times. To every *thing there is* a season and a time to every purpose under the heaven (Ecclesiastes 3:1). God's ultimate goal for us is to give us an expected end (Jeremiah 29:11).

These people play an intricate role in commandeering this fete. The first side of this story is we see with the naked eye that our friend's spouse or companion is not what we would want for them or we may believe they are not right for them and then they begin to show signs of inadequacies. But by faith, we should see them through the finished work of Christ on the cross, striving to become the person God predestined them to be. I know this can sometime be a hard task to accomplish, but we are striving for Christian maturity and not be involved with situations similar to Peyton Place. I know, I'm dating myself now.

This may not be done in our time but at God's appointed time. The question is: What are we doing to help or encourage the situation in a positive way? Of course, we are praying (right?), but are we sharing ways to improve the person in need, or are we gossiping about it? Who does the latter of this help? We've all at sometime or another been guilty of this. Hmmm, compassion! It can go a long way, if we would just operate in it.

Now the flip side of that same situation shows that it's their nature to be difficult, and not Christlike, and show no intentions or signs of ever changing. In this case, I am reminded that all things will work together for our good (Romans 8:28, paraphrase). God knows exactly what trial, tribulation, and/or circumstance is necessary to get our loved ones to their expected end. You see, it often takes a tragedy or life-changing decision to get some of us moving in God's perfect will for our lives. So whatever situation you are faced with, know if God brought you to it, he will also see you through it. Your deliverance comes after your obedience to God. You may want to take a few minutes to marinate on that one. We will talk a little more about obedience in the final chapter. Stay tuned!

The point I'm trying to convey here is that we, as creative beings, must be careful what we say out of our mouths. Proverbs 18:21 instructs us that both life and death are in the power of the tongue. Maybe the book of Matthew explains it a little better in chapter 12 verses 36–37 (KJV).

> But I say unto you, that every idle word that men shall speak, they shall give an account thereof in the day of judgement. For by thy words thou shalt be justified, and by thy words thou shalt be condemned.

We should always strive to speak life to all situations. If we are speaking anything contrary to glorifying our heavenly Father or edifying our brothers and sisters, we are just speaking idle words that will be judged. I don't know about you, but I really don't want to stand before a just God trying to explain why I talked about this person or that person. We have a choice in what we say and how we say it. And please, let's stop making excuses for gossiping and tearing down others. If you are not the one doing the talking, guess what, you are still just as guilty. If you continue to listen to it, be it out of fear of not being honest with the person or because your itchy ears want to hear it, you are no different from the one spreading the gossip. Been there, done that, and bought the tee shirt. We must act out of compassion and with Holy Ghost boldness and do as the Bible instructs us; do good and hate evil. Our soul depends on that very truth. Man has no place to put you, but God does. Fear God, not man. Stand for righteousness sake and stop thinking these so-called little sins won't affect our relationship with a holy God. The concept or principle is relatively simple—*speak life*, be justified, speak death, *be condemned*. Got it?

All of us, at some time or another, have experienced

something that has caused us pain. If we would only remember what it felt like at that particular time, just maybe we could extend a little compassion someone else's way. Most pain has purpose, and when you're in Christ, it (the pain) will work for your good. Take a moment to look beyond the next person's faults so you can tap into their need to be healed, delivered, and set free from some things. Let's be an extension of Christ in this earthly realm and help those that may be help-less. Remember our ministry of reconciliation is to be extended to the brokenhearted, the blind, the poor, and those that are held captive. Surely you've been one of these people spiritually before, I know I have. But I thank God for continuing to look beyond my faults and meet each one of my needs to be whole!

Patience is another reason God strategically places people in our lives. Have you ever met someone that did not rub you the right way? You can't seem to put your finger on it, but something just doesn't sit right? Not only is this an opportunity to show compassion but to also exercise patience. We must be patient with what we may see as shortcomings or faults in others. My pastor (Apostle Mattie H. Johnson) always says "You never know what a person has been through."

Therefore, we really shouldn't judge them based on what we see.

In our text, we see that Jesus not only endured sufferings for our sakes, but neither did He try to retaliate against those who judged Him erroneously. The scripture points out that we were called, but called unto what? We were called that we *should* follow in Christ's footsteps (verse 21). He paved the way in which we are to treat one another. He even set the standard on how we should respond to sufferings and false accusations. We can't control other people's actions, but we most certainly can control our response. God is definitely looking at how we respond to situations, and the response determines our position in him. The text goes on to say that Jesus never once participated in a tic-for-tac scenario with his accusers, but rather, he *committed* himself to him that judgeth righteously (verse 23). Who or what are you committed to? Do you trust God enough to know that he will perfect that which concerneth you and will not forsake the works of his own hands (Psalm 138:8)? Let's take this another step further and look a little deeper at some of the attributes of Christ specifically as our example setter. First, Christ loved God so much that he never deviated from God's will for his life, even though he knew God's will for him meant death. Secondly, Christ loved God's people so much that he gave his life for us. And lastly, Christ had compassion for those he came in contact with on a daily basis. On the night Christ was to be betrayed, he knew Judas was the one who would betray him, but he chose not to expose Judas. Lesson: Just because you have the power to do something doesn't necessarily mean you have the authority to do it. Both power and authority come from God. God will instruct us when to expose and when not to expose something. This is why it is imperative that we are sensitive to the Holy Spirit. We never know how much damage we are doing to a person when we do something for the sake of being right. Christ would have been right in telling Judas he was the one, but what parts in history may have changed as a result of it? All things must go according to God's will and not our wills.

So we see in 1 Peter chapter 2 that Jesus was sent for a number of reasons, but one of them was to be an example to us. Christ left his roadmap for us to follow. Just as he suffered for our sakes, we should suffer (bear the infirmities of the weak) for others. Just as

Christ bore the sins of the world, we too should show compassion and have patience toward the lost. Also, in verse 25, we find that Jesus is the shepherd and the bishop of our souls. This means that he not only watches over our souls, but he also guards our souls. Who wouldn't want the One who is, the One who was, and the One who is still to come to watch over and keep them from danger, seen and unseen? How sweet it is to have Jesus lord over our lives! There is no better caretaker I know on this side of Jordan.

Point Six

A Life of Holiness

I beseech you therefore, brethren, by the mercies of God, that ye present your bodies a living sacrifice, holy, acceptable unto God, which is your reasonable service. And be not conformed to this world: but be ye transformed by the renewing of your mind, that ye may prove what is that good, and acceptable, and perfect, will of God.

Romans 12:1–2 (KJV)

In the tenth chapter of Romans, at the tenth verse, we find that with the heart man believes unto righteousness and with the mouth confession is made unto salvation. What exactly does all this mean? It means that the very fabric in which you are made lets you know that there is someone greater and more powerful than you. We are only able to believe this truth by faith. And it is by faith that we are able to confess with our mouths that Jesus Christ, the Son of God, made the way for us to return unto him. This is also true with salvation, for it is by confession and belief that we are saved. Everyone who accepts Christ as Lord and Savior has an obligation to walk this walk by faith and live a lifestyle of holiness, which brings us to our meditation scripture.

Here, Paul is making a plea to the believers at Rome to basically give of themselves unselfishly toward the cause of salvation. Paul's plea to the Church, both then and now, is that we give our life unto God and to his cause as a sacrifice. Paul has given us three areas in which we are to present our sacrifices. Paul's first plea is that we present our bodies a *living* sacrifice. His second plea is that we present our bodies as a *holy* sacrifice. And his final plea is that we present our bodies as an *acceptable* sacrifice unto to God. Before we examine these different types of sacrifices, let's be certain we understand what sacrifice mean. Sacrifice is an act of offering to deity something precious, or destruction or surrender of something for the sake of something else. In layman's terms, sacrifice is giving up something of yours for someone else; the act or will of unselfishness. God knew we would have issues with this simply due to our nature and makeup. The body was born into sin and shaped in iniquity; therefore, it wants what it should not have. And that is normally what separates us from a holy God, the things of this world. That is also why the Bible teaches us not to have our hearts on the treasures of this world, things that are temporal, but instead, we should have our hearts fixed on treasures that are above and eternal.

When we think of sacrifices during times of old, we equate the term with something that had to die, namely, an animal, to take the place of something else. Although there were many different types of sacrifices that included sacrificing people, animals, and the like, the only kind that pleased God was the sacrifice of a pure animal without spot or blemish. Today, God is still looking for the sacrifice that is alive, pure, and acceptable.

Living Sacrifice

Paul is asking the Church to present their bodies a living sacrifice. How do we accomplish this fete? First we must know what not to do in order to know what to do. Romans 6:13 (KJV) says, "Neither yield ye your members as instruments of unrighteousness unto sin: but yield yourselves unto God, as those that are alive from the dead, and your members as instruments of righteousness unto God."

We are not to relinquish or give up to the enemy our will to do that which is right so that our flesh can be satisfied for the moment. Our bodies, once we've been reconciled back to God through Jesus' sacrifice, should be committed to do the work of God. You see, the scripture says we are now alive from the dead, which means our spirit man was dead but now lives because of Christ Jesus. We are to give or present ourselves to and for God, as those whose spirit were once dead but now live. We are to live with a spirit of thanksgiving, a spirit of gratitude, and a spirit of fervency to fulfill God's purpose for our lives. Be a living sacrifice unto God, not a sacrifice that is dead or dormant!

Holy Sacrifice

Paul is asking the Church to present their bodies as a holy sacrifice. Holy is a word that we aimlessly like to toss around because it sounds good and we believe if we say it people will believe we are. Being holy is who you confirm you are by your lifestyle. It's not in words but in deed. Leviticus 10:10 (KJV) declares, "And that ye may put difference between holy and unholy and between unclean and clean." Here, God is instructing Aaron to make a difference between what is holy and not holy and what is clean and not clean. One of the priests' main jobs was to teach the people, and more importantly, to lead by example. We find that earlier in this same chapter, Aaron's sons weren't being obedient to God in doing what they were asked. Therefore, they were subject to the consequences of their actions. Aaron's two sons allowed some *thing* to contaminate that which was holy, making it unholy. This caused distance between them and God, and will cause distance between us and God if we allow it. God is attracted to a sacrifice, but it's only a sacrifice when it has been presented willingly and blameless. We don't want to be like Aaron's two sons, offering strange fire in our sacrifice. Now that's another Bible-study lesson!

When God declares a thing, it is so. Who are we to change what God wants. If he wants us holy, don't you think he would make provisions for us to live holy? If we were made in his image and likeness, and he is holy, wouldn't that make us holy as well? Holiness is available to us, and we ultimately have it if we want it. We just have to work at keeping it. How do we remain holy? We constantly stay before a holy God. We can't go to God any kind of way but except through worship. We can't worship unless we begin to thank and praise him for who he is, and we can't praise him until we realize what we used to be and who we've become because of him, thereby, repenting of our old nature and way of life. I believe I may have a few witnesses with me on this one. Since you don't want to believe me, let's look at Leviticus 10:3, (KJV) which says, "Then Moses said unto Aaron, This is it that the LORD spake, saying, I will be sanctified in them that come nigh me, and before all the people I will be glorified. And Aaron held his peace." The place of sacrifice must remain holy, blameless, so we can stay close to God. Are you living holy?

Acceptable Sacrifice

Paul is asking the Church to present their bodies as an acceptable sacrifice. Just as we can't enter into the presence of God any kind of way, we can't offer him any kind of sacrifice either. God has always required our best. Why? He has always given *us* his best, even his only begotten Son. Genesis 4:3–7 (KJV) records it this way:

> And in process of time it came to pass, that Cain brought of the fruit of the ground an offering unto the LORD. And Abel, he also brought of the firstlings of his flock and of the fat thereof. And the LORD had respect unto Abel and to his offering. But unto Cain and to his offering he had not respect. And Cain was very wroth, and his countenance fell. And the LORD said unto Cain, Why art thou wroth? And why is thy countenance fallen? If thou doest well, shalt thou not be accepted? And if thou doest not well, sin lieth at the door. And unto thee *shall* be his desire, and thou shalt rule over him.

This is an account of Cain and Abel, sons of Adam and Eve, offering to God their sacrifice. Cain offered his best, which was the fruit of the land. Abel offered his best, which was the firstling of his flock. They both offered unto God that which they thought would be pleasing unto God, but only one of the sacrifices was acceptable, Abel's. People always wonder why Cain's sacrifice was not suitable to God. It wasn't so much what Cain was offering as it was the intent behind the offering. Cain was making an offering to God when his heart wasn't right. God cannot and will not accept any type of sacrifice. Our sacrifices must be pure, without spot or blemish. When we offer to God a sacrifice of praise, it should not be with the preconceived notion that we're going to receive a gift from him. We should praise him because he's worthy, not because of what he holds in his hands. When we sacrifice our time or talents for God, it should not be because we know there's a blessing to receive from it. I'm not saying you won't be blessed or that you shouldn't expect a blessing, I'm just saying we should do things for God simply because we love him and because he is God.

In order for us to present our bodies a living sacrifice, we must allow the Word of God to wash us and cleanse us from our old attitudes and characteristics. Only the Word of God and the workings of the Holy Spirit can bring about change in a Christian's life.

How do we allow this change to occur? Psalms 91:1 gives a hint on where we might begin, and it reads, "He that dwelleth in the secret place of the most High shall abide under the shadow of the Almighty." We must get so close to God that we begin to mirror the One who sits at his right side, Jesus. In order to get close to him, we must dwell where he is. So where do we find him? We will find him in the secret place. To dwell in a place means to establish it as a personal, intimate place. This particular place should be set aside just for you and yours. But in this case, the case to which we are referring, it should be just for *you*. God specifically calls this particular dwelling place a secret place. Why do you believe it's a secret? Well, Proverbs 25:2 (KJV) tells us, "It is the glory of God to conceal a thing: but the honour of kings to search out a matter." The things we discuss with God, he conceals all of that information. And the things God reveals to us while in the secret place aren't mentioned to anyone, ever. Because of this, we can trust God and spend even more time in that secret place.

What can be derived from being in the secret place of the Most High? And how do we abide under the shadow of the Almighty? When we dwell in the secret place, we receive protection, refreshing, and restoration. God is bidding us to come and be transformed into the image of his Son Jesus. But why won't we go, or at least not consistently? For me, the answer was clear. I allowed the cares of this world to run interference between me spending time in the presence of God and studying his Word.

Now I really don't want you to get things twisted and think that this seasoned Christian just all of a sudden began turning away from God, on the contrary. We must keep in mind that the enemy is subtle and he makes most things happen gradually, especially for the seasoned folks. And yes, I said "a turning away" from God. Make no mistake, if you are not pressing toward the mark of the high prize, which is in Christ Jesus, and you're not praying or studying the word, you are in fact turning away from God and turning to something or someone else. And as I said earlier, God is indeed a jealous God, and he has every right to be so. He has work for us to do here in this earth realm, and we cannot get it done, deviating from the course he has set before us. Anyone who is not feeding and strengthening their spirit man is susceptible to turning away from God. Once you are born again (spiritual rebirth and regeneration), it is your spirit that should be leading you in all godly truths and not your flesh (earthly satisfactions). This is why it is extremely important that you develop, cultivate, and practice being in God's presence.

Now what happens when we don't spend quality time in the presence of God? First, we open ourselves to fall prey to the tactics and schemes of the enemy. Secondly, we lose power to fight the good fight of faith. And thirdly, we run the risk of operating in our own fleshly desires and abort the purpose and plan of God. We also slowly lose our identity as an ambassador of Christ and take on worldly characteristics. When we take on worldly characteristics, we push aside everything that is Christ centered and we begin to walk in self-centeredness. Walking in self-centeredness takes us out from the shadow of protection of God, and if we stay out there too long, He will eventually turn us over to ourselves, and nobody wants that.

To get into God's presence, simply set a time daily when there are no or very little distractions, and purpose to meet God in prayer. Begin your prayer with adoration for who God is and move into thanksgiving for what God has done and then straight into worship for God loving you so much that he gave his Son to pay a ransom so you and I can come to him through the bloodshed of Jesus. Once we have done this, ask God to remove all sin, confessed or otherwise, and to cleanse you from all unrighteousness. Remember, this is a place where you can divulge your inner most secrets and not feel ashamed or condemned. Speak openly and freely to God about *you*! After doing this, you can begin to petition God on behalf of others. Again, this is called intercession. When you feel a release in your spirit, like a weight or burden has been lifted, you may be finished, but don't forget to allow God his time. You see, prayer is two-way. We pray to God and then we listen to him. God is always speaking to us through his Word, earthly vessels, or to us personally through prayer and even in our dreams. The question is: Are we listening?

Point Seven

Thy Will Be Done

Not every one that saith unto me Lord, Lord, shall enter into the kingdom of heaven; but he that doeth the will of my Father which is in heaven.

Matthew 7:21 (KJV)

Actions speak louder than words. Many of us have been hearing this most of our lives, but it does appear to carry a lot of truth with it. As mentioned in our lead scripture, it is not what we say that will guarantee us a spot in the kingdom of heaven, but rather it is what we do that will. Please do not take this out of context. We cannot work our way to heaven in the sense that we perform good deeds and neglect the truth that the only way to the Father is through his Son, Jesus Christ. Also keep in mind that the only good deeds that are done according to God's will are the ones that will count. We are justified by faith and not by our works, which means there was nothing we did to warrant the gift of Jesus dying on the cross, nor did we do anything deserving to receive such a gift. We received this gift simply because God loves us and He made and kept a promise to the heirs of Abraham. We are so blessed to have such a loving Father.

It is very important that we spend some time under-standing what God's will is for our lives. Scripture points out in great detail God's will for his people, but God also gives us the knowledge of his will individu-ally, as well as collectively. God's will for each individual differs from individual to individual, but his will for us collectively remains the same. Let's examine scripture to find the answer for God's will for us collectively.

According to Romans 12:2, God's will is good, acceptable, and perfect, and it also has to be proven or shown by us through our daily living (paraphrased).

Jesus, our perfect example, did just that, performed God's will for all to see and hear, as well as proved it to be good, acceptable, and perfect. God's will for Jesus helped pave the way for his will for us collectively, because Jesus was able to fulfill it successfully. You see, everything Jesus died for on the cross, we have to prove that it was good, acceptable, and perfect through our living. God's will for us collectively is nothing more than us proving his Word (Jesus is the Word wrapped in flesh) is good, acceptable, and perfect (or true).

Again, actions speak louder than words. We can no longer tell a dying world that Jesus saves, we must now prove it, and we prove it through our living and through the sharing of our testimonies. The Church has let the world down with all our hypocrisy, deception, and misleading behavior. It has gotten to the point where words simply do not mean a hill of beans. Folks no longer want to hear it's going to be all right, they want to know it's going to be all right. People are hurting in so many different ways, and they don't need another cliché to get them through until they get home. What they need is a Word that has been tested, tried, and proven; they need us!

People, God's will has always been his Word (Jesus)!

As I mentioned earlier, Jesus was our greatest example. We can assuredly learn a few things from his life, especially the things which occurred just before or leading up to his betrayal and eventually his crucifixion. As we look at the events that took place in Matthew chapter 26:27, we see a profound principle come to fruition. The very first occurrence is the *preparation*" found in Matthew 26:1–56. In these verses of scripture, Jesus begins by informing the disciples once again about his destiny to be betrayed and eventually crucified (verse 2). In this reading, Jesus is being cared after by a woman with an alabaster box filled with very precious oil (verse 7). I am sure many of you recall the story, but the disciples had a problem with the woman wasting such costly oil on Jesus (verse 8–9). Sidebar: How many of you know there is nothing *wasted* in Jesus? Remember, *all* things work together for our *good*!

Jesus, referring to His destiny again, replied, "For in that she hath poured this ointment on my body, she did it for my burial" (verse 12). Here in is the lesson learned: we must be *prepared* to perform the will of God. Every child of God must go through a preparation period for the things of God, and the timetable placed on this preparation period depends totally upon us. If we rebel and run from it, it will more than likely take longer. If we procrastinate, it will more than likely take longer. If we are fearful or faithless, it will more than likely take even longer.

I do not want you thinking that this is a one-time deal. The preparation period is tied to our elevation and our destiny. Whenever we have to do something great in the sense of miraculous or mind blowing for God, guess what; there's a preparation period tied to it! The individual assignments God has given us require us to be prepared specifically by him, so that when it manifests, it will be God getting all of the glory for it and not we ourselves. Never take God's glory.

The Bible refers to another time Jesus was being prepared to do the will of his Father. The three Gospels, Matthew (3:1–17), Mark (1:1–11), and Luke (3:1–22), speak of Jesus being baptized by John the Baptist and then being immediately tempted by the enemy. Shortly after, he was ministered to by the Holy Spirit (prepared to perform God's will). The next time we hear of Jesus, he is performing all kinds of miracles and setting people free from their issues. The message in all of this is, do not try to skip out on your preparation periods. They are necessary for your elevation in ministry, as well as your elevation in everyday life. It is in the preparation periods that we are prepared for life on earth and for our life of eternity with our heavenly Father.

Many of us believe we have to get to heaven before we can experience heaven. I'm here to share with you that we don't have to wait. Once we've accepted Christ's death, burial, and resurrection, we actually have eternity living within us. I'm not saying there won't be a location change once we die, but while we are here on this side, God expects us to live life in abundance. He set it up that way! On this side, we will have to endure hardship, pain, and suffering. On this side, we will cry, but in the new location, there will be no more crying, no more pain, and no more death.

Yes, we can have heaven on earth, but just as it is with God's promises, so it is concerning his will. We must be obedient! Obedience to God will often mean giving up something that makes us feel secure, and it is usually a false insecurity at best. Think about it, what is the one thing that keeps us from being obedient to God? Plainly put, it is sin. When we sit down and really think things over, we will see that it is only sin that hinders our obedience to a loving Father. Our will, before Christ and sometimes after we receive Christ, is selfish and sin driven. It is all about us, what we can get and how fast we can get it. Our will is sinful, and the body is just the instrument in which sin uses to manipulate the act. This is why it is important that our mindset changes to reflect the Word of God. We should be tired of doing things our way and hasten to do things God's way.

Do you want to live a life that is filled with perpetual blessings? Are you tired of living and participating in a mediocre life? If you are a child of the King, then your answers should be yes to these questions. God did not intend for us to live an average life, but he came that we might have life and life in abundance: spiritual abundance and natural abundance. When we embrace God's purpose, we gain his power. We gain power to get wealth. We gain power to tread upon serpents. We gain power to speak life and not death. We gain power to prophesy to the dry things in our life so they can live. We gain power to be everything God has preordained and predestined us to be. If you lack knowing the will of God, ask and he will give you wisdom concerning it. But don't waste another day being stagnated and purposeless. Stand to your feet and profess that you are who God says you are and you will do what God has purposed for you to do, in the name of Jesus. Let your work here on earth be an extension of what you will be doing in eternity, worshipping and praising God. We can worship God through our obedience to him. Find your place of worship. Find your place of praise. And, please find out and perform the will of God for *your life*!

> Now the God of peace, that brought again from the dead our Lord Jesus, that great shepherd of the sheep, through the blood of the everlasting covenant, make you perfect in every good work to do His will, working in you that which is well pleasing in His sight, through Jesus Christ: to whom be glory for ever and ever.
>
> Hebrews 13:20–21 (KJV)

Amen!

Bibliography

Webster's New Collegiate Dictionary, G&C Merriam
Company, Copyright 1979

About the Author

Rev. Patricia Deloatch is a native Washingtonian, along with her husband Deacon Bill DeLoatch. Ordained in March 2004, Rev. DeLoatch is known for her unique, animated, down-to-earth teaching/ preaching style. Her passion is to disciple mankind through the Word of God and a holy lifestyle to advance the kingdom of God.